I want world
sympathy in
this battle of
Right against
Might
Dandi M.K.Gandhi
5.4.'30

A great man of India, Mohandas Karamchand Gandhi inspired his countrymen, then under British rule, to unite in a bid for freedom that would make India an independent democracy.

Gandhi had a strong sense of right and wrong. He was a man of character who encouraged people to act on behalf of the greater good.

The famous Indian poet, Rabindranath Tagore (1861–1941), called him a "mahatma," meaning "great soul." French writer Romain Rolland (1866–1944) said Gandhi was as stubborn as a mule, but a "sacred mule."

During his lifetime Gandhi's countrymen affectionately called him "Grandpa." After his death, they reverently referred to him as sadhu, which means "saint," and worshipped him as a mahatma.

So what is Mohandas Karamchand Gandhi's story? You can see it in the pages and the pictures of this book.

Mason Crest Publishers, Inc.
370 Reed Road
Broomall, Pennsylvania 19008
866-MCP-BOOK (toll free)

Published in association with
Grimm Press Ltd., Taiwan

1 3 5 7 9 8 6 4 2

Library of Congress Cataloging-in-Publication Data:

on file at the Library of Congress.

ISBN 1-59084-143-3
ISBN 1-59084-133-6 (series)

Great Names

GANDHI

Mason Crest Publishers
Philadelphia

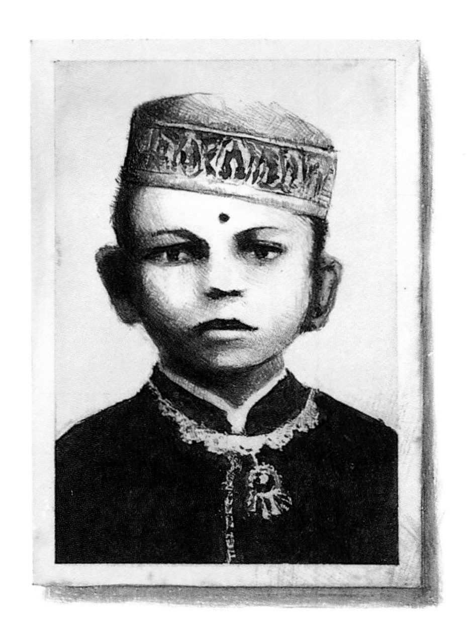

This is Mohandas Gandhi when he was seven years old.

India had been under British rule for about 200 years when Mohandas Gandhi was born in 1869.

Located at the southern end of Asia, India was an ancient country with a rich cultural heritage. Despite its sophisticated poems and flourishing art, the country did not have a unified government. This left the immense land vulnerable to foreign invasion. Great Britain, the last country to conquer India, became prosperous while the Indians were ill treated and very poor. Most could not read or write. They were poverty stricken and oppressed.

Gandhi was born into a Hindu family. There were thousands of castes and subcastes in India. They were grouped loosely into four classes, or *varnas,* a word derived from the Sanskrit for "color." At the top of the hierarchy were the Brahmans, who were priests and scholars. Then came the Kshatriyas, warriors and rulers. Next were the Vaishyas who were merchants, traders, and farmers. The artisans and laborers, called Sudras, were last. The lowliest, ranked beneath the Sudras, were called "untouchables." Gandhi called them the Harijans, or "children of God."

Since Gandhi's family sold groceries, they belonged to the Vaishyas. Gandhi was born in Porbandar, the capital of a small principality in Gujarat on the seacoast of western India. He spent his childhood there until he started attending primary school. When he was seven years old, his family moved to Rajkot, which was far away from the coast.

The newly wedded Gandhis were like a pair of children.

Couples married very young in India. Gandhi was 14 years old and in his second year of middle school when he married 13-year-old Kasturbai. Being so young, they were both headstrong and often quarreled.

Most Hindus were against the killing of livestock and did not eat meat. As a young man, Ghandhi, along with his friends, tried to prove they were men. Gandhi proved his manliness by eating meat, smoking, and stealing. He once stole a gold bracelet from his brother and sold it for money, but his conscience bothered him. He felt so bad about what he did that he told his father. His father did not scold him. Instead, he cried. From then on, Gandhi decided to follow his conscience in all things.

Rajkot, where the Ghandi family lived, was a small, bustling city. Rows upon rows of shabby board dwellings surrounded the temples where the Hindus worshipped. The streets were narrow and crowded. Unskilled laborers, known as coolies, struggled to pull carts under the burning sun. Vendors squatted under the artificial shade of large umbrellas while they sold their wares.

The young Gandhi, who was still studying in middle school, liked to wander the streets after class, but forbade his young wife from stepping outside their gate. Later in life, he said he was deeply ashamed of the unfair way he treated Kasturbai. A very emotional Ghandi said their "childhood marriage" was "two kids who knew nothing of the world thrown into the ocean of life."

After he graduated from middle school, Gandhi decided to study law in England, but his mother worried about the temptations of the distant land. The leaders of the subcaste to which Gandhi's family belonged called the trip a violation of the

Gandhi, 19 years old, wore Western clothing when he studied in London.

Hindu religion. Finally, Kasturbai sold her jewelry to fund his studies. His brother agreed to pay Gandhi's living expenses so he could follow his dream.

After Gandhi arrived in England, he dressed like an English gentleman. He refused to admit being inferior and quickly defended himself against insults.

While abroad, Gandhi witnessed the prosperity of England. He strolled through Needle Street, the financial center of London at the time. A hub of eight other roads, Needle Street was crowded with pedestrians and vehicles. The tall Royal Exchange stood magnificently on the street. Gandhi was deeply impressed by the affluence of the place.

After studying four years, Mohandas Gandhi graduated. Now a barrister, he returned to India to set up his practice. He hung out his shingle and became a practicing attorney. Unfortunately, he was shy and lacked self-confidence. This made him tongue-tied in court. So his prospects of continuing as an active lawyer were dim.

His legal practice failing, Gandhi was at a loss about what to do until a company run by a Muslim asked him to go to South Africa to settle some legal matters. Gandhi grabbed the opportunity to seek his personal advancement.

South Africa was also under British control. The majority of its population was black. But Gandhi soon discovered that the many Indians working there as coolies suffered under white control.

As a lawyer in South Africa, Gandhi wore carefully pressed Western suits, rode in first-class trains, and was no different from other young professionals in the area.

As a young man, Gandhi dressed like any Western businessman.

But South African law stipulated that Indians from Asia may not ride in first-class train compartments with whites and may not eat in the same restaurants. Furthermore, they were not allowed to walk on the sidewalks. Only whites were allowed on the sidewalks.

Once, Gandhi had to travel by train to a faraway place to transact business. He bought a first-class train ticket. Nothing happened when the train started out in the night, but when it later arrived at a small station, a white person embarked and discovered the small, thin Asian riding first class. The white person called the police, who threw Gandhi with his luggage and coat onto the station platform.

Gandhi was very angry. Refusing to ride third class, he shivered the whole night on the platform. He thought of many things during that cold night. He thought the racial discrimination in South Africa was unjust. Such an unjust law should be abolished. He felt that he should fight for the human rights of Indians living in South Africa. This was a cause for which he could fight.

Gandhi started to discuss the problem with whites, blacks, and Indians who had a sense of justice. He took part in assemblies, made speeches, and wrote articles. He quickly became known in South Africa as an Indian lawyer fighting for human rights.

Gandhi's inspiration to lead a simple life came from the book *Unto This Last* by the English writer and social reformer John Ruskin (1819–1900). Ruskin said in his

As Gandhi became more concerned with the rights of other Indians, he no longer looked like a Westerner.

book that the coin in one's pocket is useful only when one's neighbor doesn't have it. It would be useless to one if the neighbor didn't want it.

At the age of 36, Mohandas Gandhi set up a farm at Phoenix near Durban. He advocated a simple life and no longer wore Western suits.

Gandhi fought for the human rights of Indians living in South Africa. The Indians there admired and respected him. As a result, he decided to settle down there. In 1896, Gandhi traveled to India to bring his wife and daughter to South Africa. During his short stay, he spoke at public meetings denouncing South Africa's racial discrimination. This angered South African whites.

When he landed at Durban with his wife and daughter in 1897, Gandhi was assaulted and nearly lynched by a white mob. They first threw eggs, stones, and bricks at him. Then they hit and kicked him. Gandhi held tight onto some iron handrails near him. His body gradually sagged to the ground. Fortunately, when the local police commissioner's wife passed by, she chased away the whites attacking Gandhi. Using her parasol to fend off the stones and bricks, she saved his life.

The British government wanted to arrest the guilty men, but Gandhi refused to prosecute his assailants. He said that violence should not be used against violence, since that would only breed hatred. He advocated the use of sincerity and moving

adversaries to lay down their arms. This was his *ahimsa,* his spiritual belief that led to his practice of nonviolent noncooperation against British rule.

He knew that for the South African government to treat Indians fairly would require long-term struggles. To prepare for the struggle and to build up energy, Gandhi set up a farm that became a precursor of the famous *ashrams* or ideal communities. He encouraged everyone to lead a simple life, plant their own grain, and take care of their necessities while serving other people. He called this a constructive or self-supporting program.

Gandhi also designed his own clothes made of coarse cloth. He carried a shoulder bag and a bamboo stick. These were symbolic of the long road ahead that was to be traveled on foot.

Mahatma Gandhi did many things for the Indians who suffered from racial discrimination. He led protests against British rule and consistently persisted in nonviolence. He and his followers won victory after victory. He called the strength that originates from nonviolence *satyagraha,* "devotion to truth."

Gandhi was often arrested and jailed because he assumed responsibility for the actions of his followers. He often even asked to go to jail, for it was there he felt the happiness of being able to suffer as his compatriots suffered. He found jail spiritually uplifting and free.

In 1913, the British government published two laws. One announced that all Indians in South Africa must register at police stations, be fingerprinted, and be issued a registration card. The other law pronounced that to be legal, all marriages had to be of the Christian faith. Marriages of other religious faiths were not recognized.

These laws led to work strikes among Indian miners, and they also aroused the indignation of Indian women.

This time Gandhi organized a satyagraha march in which none carried a registration card. People lined up and started out from one South African province and marched to another in protest. More and more people joined in the march. Later, 50,000 Indian laborers stopped working. The British arrested people nonstop

When he was 46, Mahatma Gandhi and his wife, Kasturbai, returned to India. The couple is dressed in traditional Indian clothing.

and the jails overflowed. Ultimately, the government softened its stance and agreed to rescind the two unreasonable laws. Gandhi won final victory.

Mahatma Gandhi taught that nonviolence and fear are two contradicting concepts. Nonviolence is a lofty good and fear is entirely opposite. Nonviolence arises out of a sense of love. Fear arises out of a sense of hate. Nonviolence takes upon oneself the suffering of others. Fear, on the other hand, makes others suffer.

When World War I broke out in 1914, Gandhi's 21-year fight in South Africa ended. His South African exploits increased his fame in India. When he returned to India with his wife, his country's people had high expectations. They invited Gandhi to speak at many different meetings.

He rode in third-class train compartments so he could be with the people during his travels throughout the country. He visited Hindu and Muslim families to listen to their concerns.

He noticed the utter poverty of the Indian peasants and workers as well as the animosity between Hindus and Muslims. It bothered him that an ancient nation like India had lost its dignity because of prolonged foreign rule. He detested the dirt and chaos in the lives of the Indians. He recognized the need for thorough reform.

Gandhi soon discovered that what he wanted to do in India was a hundred times more difficult than what he had done in South Africa. Many of the British colonies around the world were clamoring for independence. If India was to acquire freedom,

Gandhi (left) at the age of 50; Rabindranath Tagore (middle), a Nobel Prize winner; Brig. Gen. Reginald E.H. Dwyer (right) of the British army.

it must become independent. However, Gandhi did not know if the country was ready for freedom. Yet he hoped that India would become a new country with independence, dignity, and unity.

Mahatma Gandhi was respected and admired by Indians. More and more people became his followers. He launched a satyagraha campaign, which had been so effective in South Africa, in search of compensation for the exploited peasants. He used fasting as a weapon to help the workers increase their meager incomes. The Indian poet, Rabindranath Tagore, now respectfully called him mahatma.

In 1919, the British announced the Rowlett Acts, which empowered authorities to impose long prison terms without trial on people suspected of rebellion. It provoked Gandhi into announcing another satyagraha struggle in protest of such a law that disregarded human rights. More than 20,000 Indians attended a meeting in Amritsar on April 13, 1919. Acting on the orders of British army commander, Brigadier General Reginald E. H. Dwyer, British soldiers opened fire at the meeting and killed more than 300 people. More than a thousand were wounded. History records this as the Massacre of Amristar. Dwyer was later removed from command and tried.

Gandhi was deeply upset by the massacre. He launched a “Noncooperation Movement” in which Indians would not work for the British, refused to pay taxes, and refused to wear British-made clothes. It brought the British economy to its knees. He also encouraged Indians to weave their own cloth and wear the clothes they made from it.

Gandhi was frequently in jail. Jails confined his physical being but could not restrain his mind.

The Noncooperation Movement spread quickly in India. Even Gandhi acquired a loom and wove up to an hour every day. The loom became a sign of the Noncooperation Movement. Many followed Gandhi's example. The whole of India resounded with the sound of looms in motion.

The Noncooperation Movement made the British government jittery. They started arresting so-called rebellious elements. Gandhi told his followers time and again not to oppose arrest with violence because the Noncooperation Movement was peaceful and should adhere to the principle of nonviolence. However, in February 1922 in Chauri Chaura, United Provinces, 22 Indian officers were massacred in their police station by a mob of protestors who set fire to the building and prevented those trapped inside from escaping the flames.

Gandhi was upset by the news and ordered an immediate stop of the Noncooperation Movement. When asked why he stopped such a powerful protest and lost the chance of throwing out the British once and for all, Gandhi said that since his followers had started using violence, the Noncooperation Movement lost its significance.

He turned himself in to the British government and asked them to imprison him. They sentenced him to six years in jail. Without complaint, he walked calmly into prison. After two years, he was released because of a serious illness.

The Noncooperation Movement stopped, but a new disturbance was appearing in India. The Hindus and the Muslims never got along. The Muslims were in the minority, and Gandhi frequently admonished the Hindus to be tolerant and forbearing toward the Muslims.

Mahatma Gandhi had been fasting for three weeks. The little girl sitting beside his bed is called Indira. She later became Prime Minister of India.

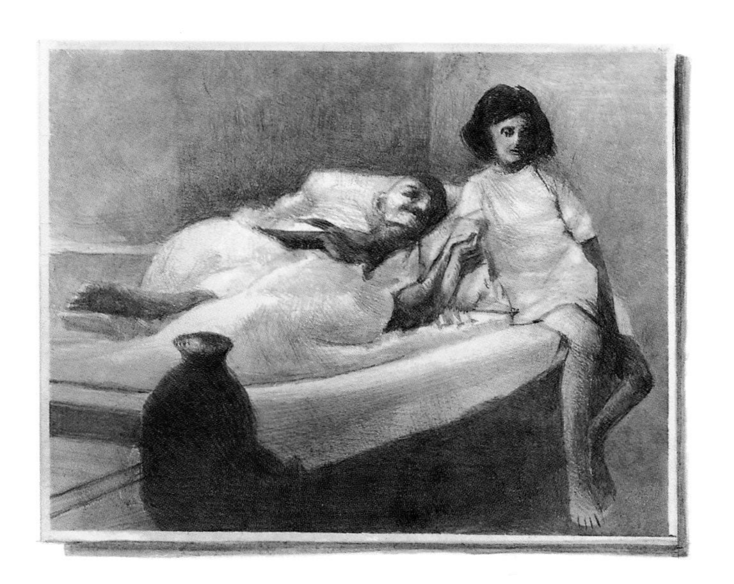

The future India, according to Gandhi, would call for Hindus and Muslims to live in cooperative harmony. After Gandhi was released from jail, conflicts between Hindus and Muslims became increasingly serious. Revengeful killings occurred frequently. Gandhi traveled to many places where he sometimes stayed in Hindu homes and sometimes in Muslim ones. He counseled harmony between them. They seemed willing to listen to him.

Regretfully, those places that Gandhi did not visit still had many revengeful killings. He was deeply pained and decided to fast in the hope that the Hindus and Muslims would be persuaded to stop their killings. Unexpectedly, they agreed to reconcile for Gandhi's sake. This was something that no one but Mahatma Gandhi could achieve. He smiled a benevolent smile.

Gandhi was 57 years old in 1925. He was elected president of the Indian Congress Party. He continued to lead a simple life and never seemed to rest. Wrapped in a piece of white cloth with one end draped around the shoulder, Mahatma Gandhi went around addressing public meetings and collecting donations. He was widely loved by the people, but he was also aware of their pressing expectations. As they looked to him to lead them to independence, Gandhi continued to negotiate with the British. However, reluctant to let go of India, the British adopted a strategy of evasion, lies, and postponement.

As a result of launching mass protests, Gandhi was arrested and jailed many times. The British government consistently refused to restore freedom and independence to India.

I am familiar with the road,
It is straight and narrow.
It is as sharp as a knife's edge,
But I enjoy walking this road.
I cried when I fell,
But the Supreme Being told me:
Brave warriors never wither.

I have never doubted such promises,
Even though my weakness has caused me thousands of failures.
I have never lost my belief,
And continue to hold onto hope.
The day will come
When I will see hopes radiating brightness.
—Mahatma Gandhi

The Noncooperation Movement is undertaken to arouse the multitude's awareness of their dignity and strength. Only when they know they need not fear brutality and threats and only when they recognize their strong determination, can this movement be put to practice. —Mahatma Gandhi

Earnest suffering and courageous tolerance might even melt a heart of stone. —Mahatma Gandhi

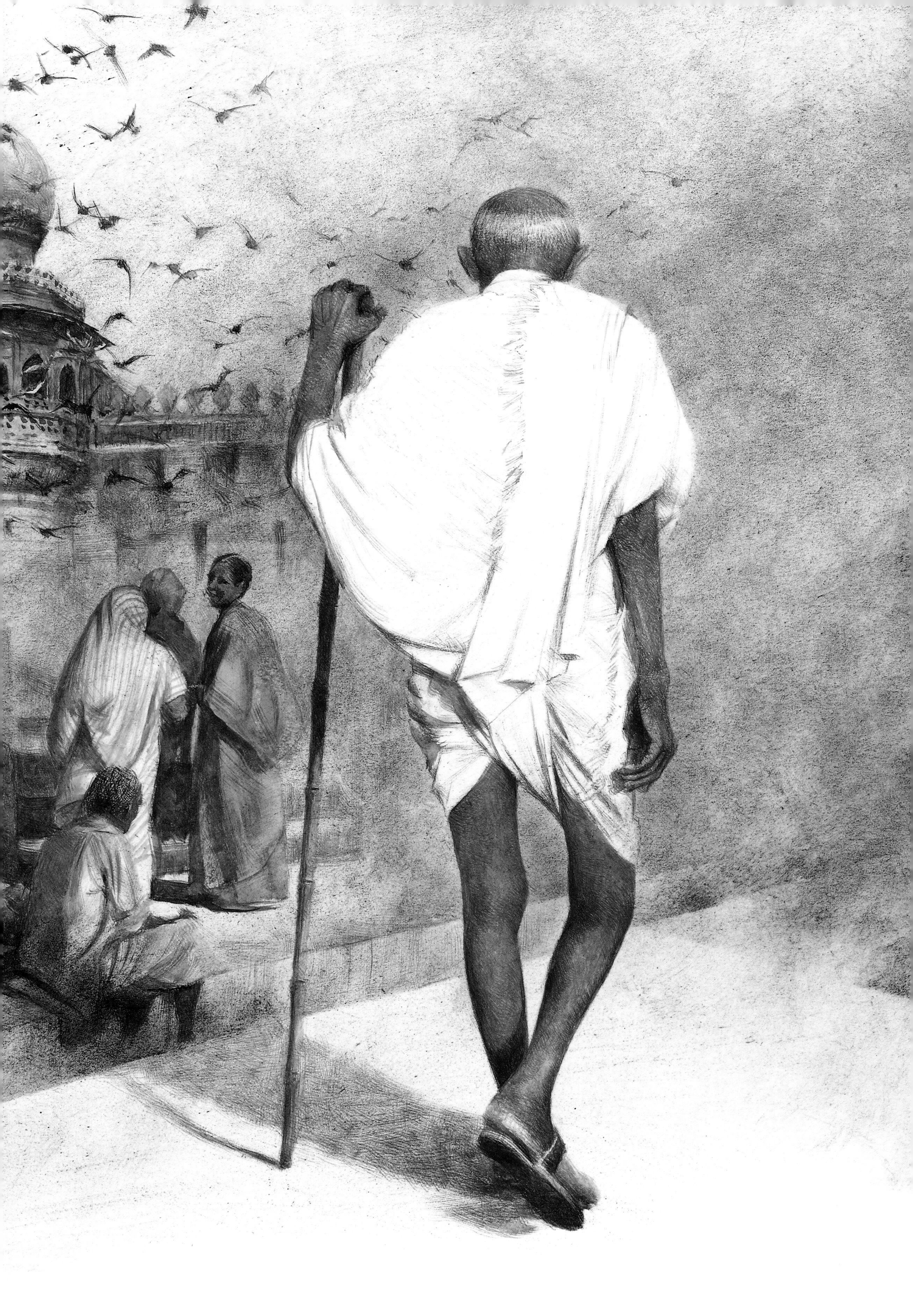

In March 1930, Gandhi announced to the public and formally informed the British government that he was embarking on his second satyagraha campaign. This time he would march with people from his ashram (religious retreat) at Sabarmati, near Ahmadabad, Gujarat, to the sea at Dandi. Once there, he and his followers would illegally pick up salt from the sands on the shores. This was the famous march against the salt tax.

Initially, a small number of people marched against the salt tax. As they marched, people joined along the way. By the time they reached the seashore, there were several thousand.

Gandhi was at the head of the marching crowd. When they arrived at the seashore, Gandhi bent and picked up handfuls of salt-sand. The marchers followed suit and bent and picked up handfuls of salt-sand.

The British government's monopoly on the sale of salt, which was heavily taxed, had long been a major source of revenue to the rulers. By picking up salt without first paying the government for it, Gandhi and his followers were breaking the law. They were telling the British that it had lost its dominion and that India no more accepted British rule.

Gandhi was arrested. Indians throughout the country rose in protest. The British government sent the cavalry to disperse the crowds. Conforming to Gandhi's principle of nonviolence, the protesters lay down on the ground. The soldiers were forced to dismount to arrest the protesters. More than 60,000 were arrested.

Another group consisting of more than 20,000 protestors led by the famous woman poet Sarojini Chattopadhyay Naidu and Gandhi's son Manilal went to a nearby salt works. Unarmed, they endured the harsh beatings of billy clubs. Those at the front were knocked to the ground, but those at their back quietly stepped forward. They gave full play to the Gandhi spirit of nonviolence.

This incident shook the world. It also softened Britain's attitude toward India. Mahatma Gandhi was released from prison and was invited to London to hold consultations on India's independence.

I want world
sympathy in
this battle of
Right against
Might.
Dandi M.K.Gandhi
5.4.'30

When they raise their fists and swing their vicious clubs to threaten us, we smile back at them. We say to them, your glaring bloodshot eyes might frighten sleepy babies. However, can they believe they can intimidate those who refuse to be intimidated? —Rabindranath Tagore

Gandhi was 63 when he went to London to attend the meeting. His warm smile charmed many. But the London conference did not bring India independence. Gandhi returned empty-handed. However, his graceful manner and loving heart made him the center of attention during the meeting.

Gandhi was getting on in years. India's independence cause was passed on to a younger generation. After returning to his homeland, he devoted himself to India's social reform. In 1939, World War II broke out and it ended in 1945.

In 1947, India gained independence. All Indians believed that it was the fruit of the decades of struggle undertaken by Mahatma Gandhi. Unfortunately, after independence, India split into two countries, the predominantly Hindu India and the predominantly Muslim Pakistan.

Gandhi was deeply distressed by the intense animosity between Hindus and Muslims in India. He was even more hurt by the division of the Indian subcontinent. He was a Hindu but he advocated fair treatment of Muslims. As a result, Hindu radicals were dissatisfied with him.

Should my belief burn with radiance in the way I had hoped it would, then even if my physical being was entombed, life would continue to exist. —Mahatma Gandhi

In the afternoon of January 30, 1948, while he was on his way to his evening prayer meeting in Delhi accompanied by two of his grandnieces, Gandhi was shot down by Nathuram Godse, a young Hindu fanatic.

Mahtma Gandhi, the man revered by all of India, fell.

After independence, the newly established government gave Mohandas Karamchand Gandhi a solemn and grand burial. India wept.

However, do they remember what was deep in Mahatma Gandhi's heart? It is true that for the sake of human rights, for equality and for independence, Gandhi suffered beatings and jail terms. But he did not let these discourage him. Deep in his heart, he knew a new India should not be merely an independent country. His greatest hope was that Indians would become hygienic, orderly, dignified, and have loving hearts. He fervently hoped that India would become a harmonious, classless country without hatred. Reality, however, prevented India from achieving this goal.

Although Gandhi did great deeds for India, his country's people disappointed him. In the end, they did not follow his goals of nonviolence. Nevertheless, Gandhi's influence can still be felt in the world—and no one has ever forgotten his loving smile.

Biographies

Author Diane Cook is a journalist and freelance writer. She has written hundreds of newspaper articles and writes regularly for national magazines, trade publications, and web sites. She lives in Dover, Delaware, with her husband and three children.

Robert Ingpen is a master illustrator who was the first Australian to win the International Hans Christian Andersen Award. His accomplishments include telling children stories with beautiful illustrations. He put to use his wealth of knowledge of the humanities and natural sciences in painting the illustrations and blended into his works his love for children, affection for the land, and respect for all living creatures.

Robert Ingpen was born in 1936 in Geelong, Australia. Ingpen's earliest work was the sketch of a shell he did when he was young. His first job, at the age of 22, was to draw and design publicity pamphlets for CSIRO, a scientific research institution.
All of his illustrations were related to various scientific research reports. The work honed his perception and established his realistic style of painting. Interestingly, Ingpen's illustrations sometimes inspired scientists to explore and study the subject at hand from new perspectives. This is where the charm of Ingpen lies.